And Heaven and Nature Sing

James R. Bjorge

CONCORDIA®

Publishing House
St. Louis

Photos by: Jay M. Steinberg—15, 22; Bruce Roberts—27, 31, 83, 95; Joan E. Rahn—67; Betty Wind— 74

Concordia Publishing House, St. Louis, Missouri
Copyright © 1977 Concordia Publishing House

MANUFACTURED IN THE UNITED STATES OF AMERICA

Library of Congress Cataloging in Publication Data
Bjorge, James.
    And heaven and nature sing.

    1. Meditations. 2. Sight-saving books.
I. Title.
BV4832.2.B52   242'.4   76-30407
ISBN 0-570-03047-1

To our five children,
Barak,
Deborah,
Nathan,
Timothy,
and Benjamin
—who love the Creator and His many creatures.

Contents

Preface

An ancient sage admonishes the lazy man with the words, "Go to the ant, O sluggard; consider her ways, and be wise" (Proverbs 6:6). An ant hill is a busy place, with every member of the colony at work. Industriousness is the way of prudence. Idleness breeds problems; so the ancient writer employs the ant to teach a lesson. "None preaches better than the ant," said Poor Richard, "and she says nothing."

We can all learn from the animal kingdom. Job says, "But ask the beasts, and they will teach you; the birds of the air, and they will tell you; or the plants of the earth, and they will teach you; and the fish of the sea will declare to you" (Job 12:7-8).

Come with me into these pages and we will attempt to receive some nurture from nature.

Go to the Ant

Go to the ant, O sluggard; consider her ways, and be wise.

Proverbs 6:6

A sandwich was being eaten in the bright sunlight, and a few crumbs tumbled to the earth. It was not long before the ants were moving in for a meal. Soon they were busily gathering the leftovers and transporting them by pushing and pulling to their food caches. It was quite a sight of industrious activity. Crumbs bigger than the ants themselves were being moved without machines under and over countless obstacles. Many times I had been annoyed by these little insects; but that day I was pausing to admire them. They work hard and cooperate as a team. They work when the working is good, and they save their product for hard times. The size of the task never seems to discourage them; they just keep at it and usually succeed.

The writer of Proverbs must have spent some time ant-watching as well as people-watching. He noted that many folk were sluggish. Now the slug is a terrestrial snail that moves painfully slow. The laziness of his fellowmen bugged the writer, and he gives them some sage advice about going to the ant and studying her ways.

The writers of Scripture have scant patience with the man who loafs his way through life and doesn't lift a finger unless he has to. Too many are afflicted with the sin of sloth. A man looking for a particular piece of lumber at the yards saw a man dressed in coveralls and asked him: "Do you work here?" "Only if I have to," was the reply.

We know that our Lord did not live a life of

contemplation and ease. He worked with His hands, and they were marked with callouses. He was a carpenter during a large portion of His earthly life. He dignified labor as an integral part of the program for humanity.

Paul knew that sweat was sweet as he stitched tents and pondered over manuscripts seeking to articulate the Gospel. He said things like this: "If any one will not work, let him not eat" (2 Thessalonians 3:10b). "It is the hard-working farmer who ought to have the first share of the crops" (2 Timothy 2:6). "Whatever your task, work heartily, as serving the Lord and not men" (Colossians 3:23).

In Longfellow's "Psalm of Life" there is a special line: "Let us then be up and doing." We were created to be creative. Work is a gift and enlarges man.

"Killing time" is a barbarous phrase for a barbarous thing. It is wasting one of God's greatest resources given to man. So let us revisit the ant and be stirred by her ways. Then back to work we go. And the big thing is not whether one's title be "sanitation engineer" or "garbage man" or "professor of theology" or "shepherd." The big thing is whether, "whatever your task," you "work heartily, as serving the Lord and not men, knowing that from the Lord you will receive the inheritance as your reward" (Colossians 3:23-24).

The Beautiful Butterfly

> For the trumpet will sound, and the dead
> will be raised imperishable, and we shall
> be changed.
>
> 1 Corinthians 15:52

If you have romped in God's big outdoors and looked for miracles, you have no doubt seen one or more. It was a day when the warm sunshine was beckoning life to come and play in the gentle breezes in the meadow. There was an expectancy that seemed to creep over all creation. Some time prior to this day a fluffy caterpillar had crawled out on a branch to die. Securing itself, it had spun a silken cocoon like a casket around its total body. Scientifically we could say it was going through the pupa stage. Something was happening in that woven tomb—death was giving way to new life. If a small boy would have tried for a sneak preview of the action inside, he would have destroyed the miracle. But nobody had interrupted the plan. So the miracle happened. The chrysalis burst open after a violent series of convulsive movements. Out came a beautiful, multicolored butterfly. It moved its wings, caught a draft of air, and soared. That which was earthbound as a caterpillar was now free to explore the sky. My heart skipped a beat as I stood and observed the empty caterpillar casket.

Butterflies are beautiful. Once Arthur Brisbane, a well-known newspaper editor of some years ago, told a tale of some caterpillars pulling an empty cocoon to its burial place. The caterpillars were dressed in black and weeping sadly. While they were on the long, somber journey, a butterfly was floating above them. While they wept, the

11

butterfly was rejoicing in his newfound freedom and life.

What a transformation! That which seemed like a sealed tomb becomes a step on the way for the butterfly. This speaks surely to an instinct that God placed in my soul. My casket shall not be a dead end for me. The casket has been conquered. Jesus, who came back from the tomb, says, "I am the resurrection and the life; he who believes in Me, though he die, yet shall he live, and whoever lives and believes in Me shall never die" (John 11:25-26). He demonstrated this that first Easter morning when He walked out of Joseph's sepulcher and started stepping down through the centuries with the good news of salvation and life.

Do you ever wonder what it will be like in the life beyond? We have no real clues of the furnishings of heaven except that it will be beyond compare. Our wildest dreams could not create the wonders God has prepared for those who love Him. Even though Scripture indicates we will be recognizable people as we now are, the glory of the imperishable nature will be a transformation as superb as the magnificent metamorphosis of the butterfly.

In the meantime, we can deliberately and patiently spin a cocoon of the threads of love and service to others around the days of our lives. For we know "that in the Lord your labor is not in vain" (1 Corinthians 15:58).

Darkness Dwellers

Every one who does evil hates the light, and does not come to the light, lest his deeds should be exposed.

John 3:20

For several years our family has collected rocks of assorted colors from places where we have been vacationing. They range from boulder-sized rocks, which caused our car springs to sag on the homeward trek, to little pebbles found on the beach of Lake Michigan. In our rock garden, petrified wood tells a story of the ages past and brain-like coral spins a tale of the sea life. And in the fun of gathering rocks we have seen a sermon from the little insects that often make their home in the dark, moist places under these rocks.

Frequently, when a rock is hoisted from its resting place, there is a frenzy of activity as the light breaks into the world of the darkness dwellers. The little, odd-looking creatures scurry in all directions when the cover is taken off their world, exposing their subway systems and their food caches. The light seems to totally unnerve them as they frantically attempt to find another dark crevice into which to crawl. The light seems to be enemy number one to these crawling creatures who have made darkness their place of habitation.

Light reveals that which is hidden. At times in our lives we become a bit frightened when we think that someone may overturn a stone on our personal landscape and disclose some loathsome crawling things which undermine our reputation and stain our Christian witness. As long as these pesky insects of the soul can be kept in darkness, we walk about as though everything is fine and dandy with us. All the while, subways of erosion and little nests of evil take their toll of our spiritual health. And we begin to like more darkness and less light.

Jesus said, "I am the light of the world; he who follows Me will not walk in darkness, but will have the light of life" (John 8:12). I guess Jesus was a rock lifter. When I walk with Him, I begin to hate things in my life about which pagans have no pangs of conscience at all. It is because of this Jesus, who turns on the light, that dirty immoralities and dusty deeds now are seen as very wrong. Cover-ups and lies cannot stand the presence of His light and they must scurry from my soul.

And the light brings a new kind of life—open and free to the dancing sun and the fresh breezes. The dampness disappears and the soil becomes a seedbed for exciting new kinds of growth. That's what happens when I let Jesus' light into all the crevices of my being. Then, too, I am free, for I have nothing to hide and the soil of my soul becomes the garden of the Spirit's new growth.

"If we walk in the light, as He is in the light, we have fellowship with one another, and the blood of Jesus His Son cleanses us from all sin" (1 John 1:7).

"I looked to Jesus, and I found
In Him my Star, my Sun;
And in the Light of Life I'll walk
Till traveling days are done."
—Horatius Bonar

Looking back can be fatal

14

Doom for the Deer

No one who puts his hand to the plow and
looks back is fit for the kingdom of God.

Luke 9:62

It was the time of year when birds were riding the northwind
to their southern haunts, squirrels were chattering and
chucking nuts into their caches for a long winter, and the
canvas of nature had been splashed with every conceivable
autumnal color. To the outdoorsman the calendar was
announcing hunting time. The fall breeze seemed to
whisper, "Go west," and so we did.

The mountains of Wyoming loomed before us with
snowcapped peaks that pierced the blanket of blue sky. The
pines stood in regal beauty as sentinels guarding the
mountain palace. Here and there against the distant
foothills were patches of yellow aspens shedding their
garment of summertime. As we camped and moved out into
the hunting area, there seemed to be a solemn hush as the
creatures of the wilderness sensed that someone was
invading their domain. The hawks were sailing high above
in the thin mountain air watching our movement.
Occasionally a startled grouse would erupt from the forest
floor when our footsteps came too close.

Suddenly a mule deer buck bolted from a thicket to our
right. He dashed into an open spot with legs like coiled
springs. There was not sufficient time even to get our rifles
to our shoulders before he disappeared into a gulley. But to
our surprise he reappeared on the other side, and before he
went over the crest of the far knoll he stopped, turned
sideways, and looked back at us. That was his undoing. He

fell victim to the hunter's bullet. There would be venison on our table that winter.

It has always been somewhat of a mystery as to why many mule deer follow this dangerous habit of stopping and looking back before they disappear from sight. Maybe they are just curious as to those preying on them. During the hunting season the backward look has been fatal for countless mule deer.

Looking back has sometimes been deadly business for mankind. We remember the story of Lot's wife as they were fleeing the wicked city of Sodom. "Lot's wife behind him looked back, and she became a pillar of salt" (Genesis 19:26). Man has often been paralyzed in the present, looking back at yesterday's failures. It is easy also to slide along today if a person glories too much in yesterday's successes. The apostle Paul knew what he was talking about when he said: ". . . forgetting what lies behind and straining forward to what lies ahead" (Philippians 3:13). Because of the power of forgiveness in Christ, we can forget the failings of yesterday and gather the fruit. We cannot live on yesterday's street corner without wasting today. God wants us to confront life with face forward.

> I look not back; God knows the wasted hours, the
>   sinning, the regrets.
> I leave them all with Him who blots the record,
>   And graciously forgives and then forgets.

Shark Jaws

Let us also lay aside every weight, and sin which clings so closely . . .

Hebrews 12:1

The gaping mouth of the great white killer shark strikes fear into the heart of man. Ever since the best-selling book and the movie spectacular *Jaws* hit the public, there has been an increasing awareness about this underwater killer. You get the feeling that a shark kills for the sheer enjoyment of it. Many have been known to stay away from beaches after seeing in the motion picture the murderous mouth lined with razorlike, pointed, triangular teeth. Respect for this tyrant of the seas is good. It would indeed be foolhardy to purposely swim in shark-infested waters. It would be like playing with dynamite, and that is not healthy!

The killer shark is big and we seem to respect size. But little things can also kill. The piranha is a species of fish in the rivers of the Amazon basin. Most are less than two feet long. But they are known for their ferocity. They have needle-like teeth and will attack any animal that enters the stream. It is not unusual for a school of piranha to strip the flesh from the legs of a horse fording a stream. And they have attacked and killed men.

Today we are focusing on big things—earthquakes, towering infernos, big sharks. While concentrating on them, we tend to forget the dangers of the termites working on the very foundations of life. The big dangers seem so well-defined, and we can see them easily. The little dangers are more difficult to detect, and they can devastate the soul very subtly.

Rain and melting snow cause small streams leading to the rivers. Erosion begins. It may seem insignificant, but a farmer knows it must be stopped even though no big loss is immediately apparent. For the cumulative effect of small rivulets is almost unbelievable. Did you know that the mighty Mississippi deposits 730 million tons of sediment into the Gulf of Mexico each year? It is the work of much small erosion along its pilgrimage through the heartland of America.

Let's make this personal. Most of us live quite comfortably with our little sins. We excuse ourselves by saying, "After all, no one is perfect. I'm only human." So we settle down with our family of little sins—a bit of gossip, a touch of envy, a trace of dishonesty, a load of indifference, a stroke of selfishness, a pinch of prejudice, and on and on. But they are not big things like JAWS. We haven't stolen our neighbor's wife, or robbed a bank, or stood for communism. We have become blind to the danger of little things. They have a devious way of ganging up on us and sapping the strength of the soul. Little sins never stay little. They grow up into full-fledged evil.

While you swim through life, remember there is more danger than just big sharks!

Where Are You Looking?

. . . and let us run with perseverance the
race that is set before us, looking to Jesus
the pioneer and perfecter of our faith.

Hebrews 12:1b-2

It was a picnic supper on a little farm nestled in the hills of
Wisconsin. We had just finished some fine steaks which had
been seasoned and sizzled over a charcoal grill. Our
Norwegian Elkhound, a massively built dog, was sprawled
out on the carpet of green grass about 20 feet from the
redwood table where we were capping off the evening meal
with some delicious dessert.

The dog knew that his time was coming next, for there
were always some scraps left for him. I gathered the bones
and leftovers on a paper plate and walked over to the waiting
pet. He sat up immediately, expectancy written all over his
face. Slowly I placed the plate in front of him, but he didn't
move. Saliva began to form in the corners of his mouth as
the aroma filled his dilating nostrils. He was now tense.
However, he was trained never to begin eating until he was
given the signal, no matter how hungry he was.

How could he resist? I often wondered. One day I believe
I learned the secret. My dog's eyes never concentrated on the
food but were always fixed directly on my eyes as he waited
for the go-ahead word. In his animal wisdom perhaps he
knew the temptation was too great unless he focused his
attention away from its allurement.

Such is a lesson of faith learned from a creature of the
Creator. I remember from Scripture that Peter learned this
lesson in another way. He and the gang were out fishing in

their boat when they saw someone approaching them on the water. When Peter saw that it was Jesus, he got so excited that he asked to come and meet Jesus on the choppy water. Jesus said, "Come." So Peter did. But the waves were increasing in size. Peter could not believe what was happening. He saw the wind roiling the water—he became afraid—he began to sink. He cried, "Lord, save me!" And Jesus did. After reading this Gospel account carefully, we discover that Peter's problem arose when he took his eyes off his source of strength, Jesus, and looked instead at the wind and the waves.

The Israelites were trudging through the wilderness for years. The vision of the promised land kept beckoning them on. Finally they reached the borders of the land flowing with milk and honey. There they were stopped for 40 years. For a generation they were denied entrance. Why? It was not that they could not possess it. The problem was that 10 of the spies sent in reported that there were giants in the land, and they would be unable to conquer them. Two of the spies said God had promised it to them and they should move in and take it. The people accepted the majority report. They concentrated on the giants rather than the God of Faithfulness who had told them it was theirs for the taking.

Where you look makes all the difference as to the way you live. Annie Johnson Flint closes one of her poems with this witness:

But I look up—into the face of Jesus,
    For there my heart can rest, my fears are stilled;
And there is joy, and love, and light for darkness,
    And perfect peace, and every hope fulfilled.

The Cat's Whiskers

Bear one another's burdens, and so fulfill
the law of Christ.

Galatians 6:2

We have not been able to resist the coaxing of our children to
have a kitten around the house. The problem is that the
kitten grows into a cat. Now, not all cats are bad, but we
once had a black one that roared around the place as though
he were a tiger. His claws left evidences of crime all over our
furniture. It was too much to overlook, and so this cat got his
walking papers. However, I must admit that perhaps I
contributed to his wild ways for I was prone to tease him by
ever so carefully rubbing his whiskers while he was
catnapping. He would awaken, shake his head violently,
and then proceed to scratch his whole face. His whiskers
were very irritable.

That word "irritable" is an interesting one. When we
hear it, we usually think of it as meaning easily annoyed or
provoked to anger, impatient, or fretful. We think of an
irritable man as one who is just an overgrown baby that
turns purple in the face and begins to scream when someone
touches his rattle. But there is another definition. Webster
says that the word in medicine means excessively sensitive to
a stimulus, and in physiology it means being able to respond
when stimulated.

In that latter sense we can positively speak of this trait
as a good one for man. As people of God, we must have the

Being sensitive to everyone's needs

23

capacity to respond dramatically to the stimuli of human needs around us. We must be so sensitive that we notice human pain, detect troubled souls, are aware of human misery.

Jesus was very "irritable." He had a quick response to human need wherever He met it. Others around Him might not see it, but He would. Remember the blind man Bartimaeus? He could not see the majestic mountains, or the intricate beauty of a flower, or a breathtaking sunset. The world was a dark prison to him. One day Jesus of Nazareth was passing by. In desperation Bartimaeus cried, "Jesus, Thou Son of David, have mercy on me." The bystanders had no response of care for this cry of a fellow human being. They were not irritable to the stimulus of suffering. All they did was to shout at the blind man, "Oh, shut up." But Jesus said, "Come here, what do you want Me to do for you?" Well, we know the outcome of the story—the blind man was healed and he glorified God.

I am glad that when I whisper a prayer, God hears, for He is sensitive to my voice. But I need to become more irritable in the right way. Unless you and I respond to the touches of human need, our nerves of sensitivity and sympathy will deaden, and we will be nothing but well-dressed corpses walking down the streets of life.

Emily Dickinson caught the mood:

If I can stop one heart from breaking,
I shall not live in vain;
If I can ease one life from aching,
Or cool one pain,
Or help one fainting robin
Unto his nest again,
I shall not live in vain.

Wisdom might even come from a cat's whiskers!

The Lecherous Leech

The leech has two daughters; 'Give, give,'
they cry.

Proverbs 30:15

Fishing for walleyes in a wonderful Minnesota lake is a great vacation sport. The bait that is usually best in the business of luring a big fish onto your hook is a shiner minnow. However, in the last few years, one of the most popular baits for walleyes is the leech. The first time my younger children saw these little creatures swimming with undulating movements of contraction and elongation they were hesitant in reaching into the bait container. When a small hand ventured into the container to grab a leech for the hook, there was a scream of surprise. The leech had grabbed the hand in the process of being caught. Needless to say, the leech did not win a popularity contest with my children.

The leech is also called a bloodsucker because of the way it lives. It is a worm that has a disklike sucker at each end. It has a mouth centered in the front sucker, and may also have small teeth.

Most leeches are parasitic. They live on someone or something else without giving anything sustaining in return. Plants may be parasitic as they attach themselves to trees and roots and steal life-giving energy. Mosses may kill the trees they attire. The word parasite, of Greek derivation, describes a tasteless trait found also among humans. It signifies a person who flatters and amuses his host in return for free meals and gifts.

Maybe it is not only the appearance of the leech that does not win our approval but more so his tactics. As a parasite he has a grasping spirit that drains life out of all that he contacts. He takes but does not give. He preys upon all his relationships.

The leech is like a hitchhiker with his thumb up, saying, "You furnish the gas, the car, attend to repairs and upkeep, supply the insurance, and I'll ride with you. But if you have an accident, I'll sue you for damages." That sounds pretty much one-sided—and it is. But that is the way of the parasite.

The prodigal son, before leaving home, was a "give me" boy. When he got things straightened around in the far country and repented of his wrong, he came back home in the willingness to serve, saying, "Let me." He made the journey from the land of taking to the land of giving. When we are constantly trying to attach ourselves to the gravy train—to the man with influence, to the position of prestige—trying to squeeze something for nothing out of life, then we become less than human with the unattractive spirit of the parasitic leech.

It's a great day when the leech, who has been going along for the free ride, climbs aboard and is willing to be a part of the sail enabling the ship to reach its destination. That ship may be your home, community, state, or nation.

Being free in the greatness of God

Pike in the Pond

If you continue in My word, you are truly
My disciples, and you will know the truth,
and the truth will make you free.

John 8:31-32

As a small boy, I did a lot of fishing in the Des Moines River. My favorite spot was where the sewage from my home community was spilling into the river. Consequently my mother was not too keen about frying the fish I caught. So I used them for another project. We had a large goldfish pond in our backyard, and I would stock it with river fish. One day I caught two large pike. I hurried home with them in a large pail of water and deposited them in the goldfish pond. Previously I had patiently trained little bluegills to swim to the surface of the water in that pond and snatch worms out of my fingers. So I thought these two pike would make spectacular pets doing what the little fish had been doing. However, the next morning my anticipation turned to dejection. The pike were nowhere in sight. Immediately I thought that the neighbor's big black cat was the culprit who had robbed me of my prized fish. Later in the day, after the hot sun was baking the earth, I was sitting by the pond feeding the bluegills when my nostrils caught the odor of foul fish. I glanced in my mom's flower garden adjacent to the pond and there they were—two dead pike. I wondered— what made them jump out of the pond? Well, who can know the reasonings of a fish? Evidently they thought they did not need to be confined to such a small pond. Their world should be much bigger. So they proceeded to jump out, seeking to find freedom. They found only death.

People are sometimes like those pike. They want to break

free of all restraints and establish their own boundary lines. Contrary to popular opinion, true freedom is not doing what we please when we please in an unmastered life style. A balloon floating in the air is not free but captive to every breeze. A ship that has no rudder is captive to the power of the waves. A person who does not live by principles is captured by the passions and whims of mind and body. Goethe said, "No one is more of a slave than he who thinks himself to be free without being so." Jumping out of the responsible life ends up in the desert of nonproductivity.

Thomas à Kempis said, "A man that hath denied himself is exceedingly free and secure." He is merely saying that a man who can deny himself is no longer captive to all his whims and desires. He is willing to live within the pond of principles. Life is that way. The pianist must accept the bondage of practice if he is to be free to perform well. The athlete who wants to be free to play his best must accept the prison of the practice field. Every person has to do his own roadwork if he wants to be free to do his best. Real freedom is found only where there is discipline, self-control, and self-denial. Derek Ibbotson, a famous track star of years ago, was asked by some friends to participate in a wild party of drinking and feasting. He refused, saying, "I am not free to do what you ask. For if I did what you ask, I would not be free to run."

Jesus wants to set us free to live the abundant life. He wants to free the mind from following the herd, from the need to hate and despise, from the need to condemn and judge. Then we shall be free to live, laugh, and love in the greatness of God.

The pike could have no real freedom outside the environment of the water. We cannot have it outside the boundaries of God's kingdom. Maybe the prayer we must pray is "Make me a captive, Lord, and then I shall be free."

Till Death Us Do Part

For this reason a man shall leave his father
and mother and be joined to his wife, and
the two shall become one flesh.

Mark 10:7-8

Few creatures of the wild are monogamous. Most males of
the animal world practice the "hit and run" policy—they are
ready at all times to breed, but do not stick around and help
raise the young ones. Their romances are brief, with no vows
of responsibility.

There are exceptions, however, in both the world of birds
and mammals. The Canadian goose is a majestically
beautiful wild fowl that practices monogamy. Separating
into pairs when they reach the breeding grounds, they
become mates for life and never part. After a ceremonial
courtship, they usually build a carefully lined nest of grass,
reeds, and down near the water. The number of eggs in a
clutch is from 5 to 11. They are brooded by the female alone.
However, throughout the 28-day incubation period the
gander stands guard and defends the nesting female with his
life.

Timber wolves seem to possess more intelligence and
morality than domesticated dogs; they mate for life and
never trespass upon one another's dens and family property.
There is a lot of education in the wolf family. The parents
are careful tutors in teaching the pups the cunning ways of
the wild. At first the parents place half-killed rodents and

Being companions not competitors

30

small game near the den. The little ones learn progressively how to catch game. Later they go into the fields with mom and dad and increase their skills in stalking, speed, coordination, and obedience.

Coyotes also exhibit much affection and fidelity between mates, although there is some uncertainty as to whether they mate for life. But it has been demonstrated frequently that the mate of a trapped coyote will often stay by its mate. The free coyote brings food to the trapped one. The male often brings food to his nursing or pregnant mate. If the mother is killed, the father brings meat to the pups.

In these examples from the animal world where monogamy is practiced there seems to be a dominant factor that is very noticeable. The mated pair share responsibilities, and they work together in raising their families. They work on the art of living together. They are not competitors but companions. Each fortifies and fulfills the other. Humans are losing this quality in their pursuit of liberation. When shared responsibility is taken out of a love relationship, the backbone is removed, and the marital union can no longer stand straight and walk tall. Perhaps we need to review the vows once again: ". . . to have and to hold from this day forward, for better for worse, for richer for poorer, in sickness and in health, to love and to cherish, till death us do part, according to God's holy ordinance; and thereto I plight thee my troth."

May the call of the wild goose quicken our pulses and stir our souls with a melody of love and faithfulness.

The Night Crawler's Dilemma

Keep yourselves in the love of God
                              Jude 1:21

It was a warm summer night, and the sky had turned on its sprinkling system. The earth was moist from the gentle shower, and the large earthworm called the night crawler was out, meandering around on the top of the soil with his friends. They came to a concrete-surface driveway and cautiously crawled across its wet and warm surface. It felt good. They spent some time there enjoying the feeling on their long stretched-out bodies. But as the dawn broke, the sun burst forth through the disappearing clouds. The water evaporated quickly, and as the concrete surface was now dry, the night crawlers experienced dissipating strength as they tried to make it back to the good earth and dive into their small burrowed holes. Their skin needed moisture. They were losing it too fast. They couldn't make it off the driveway in time. By midmorning they had shriveled up and were dead.

It happened quickly for the night crawler. Out of his environment he rapidly expired. The dinosaurs of the past were not destroyed by dragon slayers like St. George. Rather the climate changed and slowly over the decades these prehistoric monsters faded out of the picture, not because of direct attack but because of weather changes.

Man was made for the environment of God. Augustine said, "Thou hast formed us for Thyself, O God, and our hearts are restless until we find rest in Thee." If man does not live in fellowship with God, his spirit wilts. He lives half a life at the best, dead to the real life.

Jesus talks beautifully about God's care for the birds of the air and the flowers of the field. Then He tells us that we should "seek first His [God's] kingdom" (Matthew 6:33). Perhaps Jesus refers to the fact that only in the environment of God's kingdom will we experience the care and concern of the Father. A bird and a flower experience God's care as they live in the environment for which they have been created. If a sparrow one day chooses to make his home under water, would God care for him there? The bird chooses death when he is unwilling to live within the boundaries of his created purposes.

When I don't consciously live, move, and have my being in God, I am out of my environment and it spells trouble for me. I need to live in the Kingdom.

James Montgomery wrote in a hymn:

"Prayer is the Christian's vital breath,
The Christian's native air."

He knew what he was talking about. We all need the Lord, and without Him we shall do no better than the night crawler on his journey of doom.

The Snake Swallowed

O taste and see that the Lord is good!

Psalm 34:8

I was a small boy exploring the mysteries in the tall grass surrounding a swampy pond. Squishing slowly with muddy boots I observed the world of frogs, water beetles, and spiders. The red-winged blackbirds, perched on bending cattails, filled the air with song as they scolded me for entering their territory. Then I spied a battle of nerves taking place on a field of swamp grass. A large garden snake was stalking a medium-sized frog. The frog seemed paralyzed with fear as the snake slowly approached with an intent glare that seemingly hypnotized his would-be victim. With a movement that was quick as a flash of lightning, the snake encased the body of the frog in its jaws. The frog was caught! I froze in my position as I watched the snake slowly manipulate the frog in his jaws so the head of the frog faced the throat of the snake. Then the jaws of the snake began to expand, capable of a separation I never dreamed possible. The snake's teeth, sharp and curved backwards, made it impossible for the frog to escape. I thought the snake would choke over the size of his noon meal. The head and throat of the snake seemed to stretch almost to bursting, and then the frog began to slowly move down inside the cylindrical body of its enemy. The whole episode seemed laboriously cruel, but nature accepted it as a way of the swamp life.

As I reflect on this incident of preying, I can't help but think of the habit of swallowing things whole. I wonder how much satisfaction that snake had in his eating process. Certainly there could have been little taste there—just a mighty gulp. Tasting food is a great gift, adding so much pleasure to the act of eating, and the snake was missing it all.

I think God wants us to taste life—to chew it well—enjoy its savor. Geraldine Farrar, former star of the Metropolitan Opera Company, said on her 80th birthday: "So much is pressing in on human life today that they do not have time to stand still long enough to evaluate it. They gulp life and taste nothing. They eat life and have no savor." Many people are duped into thinking that the destination or arrival is the only important thing. They seem to think that striving to get there is insignificant and a necessary nuisance. Consequently they do not enjoy the fun of striving or the journey toward the destination. So we gulp down youth waiting impatiently for young adulthood. We gulp down jobs waiting for advancement. We are seen and heard racing along, without pausing to savor the present and always looking ahead to some future time.

God wants us to slow down and enjoy His creation today. Experience the taste of friendship and the goodness of God. Jesus did not just say, "At the end of the way you will find Me." Rather, He said, "I am the Way" (John 14:6). William Feather said: "Plenty of people miss their share of happiness, not because they never found it, but because they didn't stop to enjoy it."

The Flag of Feeling

Jesus wept.
John 11:35

You can usually tell the mood of a dog by the movement of his tail. There is no doubt about the fact that the tail tells a tale. Dogs are not ashamed of their feelings, and while their eyes convey so much emotion, it is the caboose that has the action. When a puppy has been punished for a misdeed, the tail promptly goes between the legs to let you know he is sorry for his offenses. If the dog is happy, he will let you know with a reckless wagging of the tail like a flag blowing in a brisk breeze. On some dogs, like a Boxer, where the tail has been cut short in puppyhood, the whole hind end of the dog shakes in abandonment. If you have had the opportunity of watching a good hunting dog, such as an Irish Setter, in the frozen position of pointing out a pheasant in hiding, you will see the tail straight and tense. The dog's emotion is one of readiness and alertness. Maybe one of the reasons we can become so attached to this member of the animal kingdom is that we know how they feel about us since they are not afraid to show it.

People often have problems in wearing their emotions. Many little boys, while having a battle with bumps and bruises, are told, "Now, don't cry, sonny; be a big man." If they hear nothing else, they will grow up thinking that big men don't cry. I once asked a group of 36 confirmation students if they had ever seen their fathers cry. Only two had witnessed this human emotion of sorrow or grief come to the surface and be expressed by their dads. Along with this repression of sadness there grows a parallel inability to let

37

people know that you really care about them in both the tragic and triumphant times of life. To be sure, you might have some powerful feelings at the gut level, but you have never let them surface so they can be seen by those you love. And what about the joy of laughter? The Gospel has given us all the ingredients for a great party, but we find it so difficult to pull it off on our faces. Smiles seem so scarce and laughter seems so shallow.

The longer I live the more I am convinced that the relationships of openness are the greatest. When we take off our masks and let the inner feelings rise to the surface, we are being genuine and this builds bridges of trust and concern.

Jesus was a popular dinner guest. A somber dead pan would never be delightful company. Children flocked to Him, and children only jump into the laps of men who know how to smile and laugh.

Jesus was moved by the moods and needs of people. He wept at the grave of Lazarus. He could feel the deep, intense agony of bereavement that gripped the family and friends. He joined them in crying. Goethe, the great German writer, confessed that as he grew older he lost the ability to weep. Too many of us do! Too many of us fail to laugh! Too many of us keep the lid on our emotions. Too many of us fail to give the gifts of smiles and tears.

Let us learn from the dog, who uses his tail to let the world know how he feels on the inside. God has given us words, and faces, and arms that can hug another—so we can be free to express the language of the soul.

Let George Do It

Let each one test his own work, and then his reason to boast will be in himself alone and not in his neighbor. For each man will have to bear his own load.

Galatians 6:4-5

Not all birds are good homemakers. In fact some are simply lousy mothers who desert their offspring before they are even born. The cowbird is such an irresponsible creature. The cowbird, which is related to the blackbirds, is frequently found near cattle. Most of the species of cowbirds build no nest, but lay their eggs in the nests of other birds when the owner of the nest is out. The cowbird then flies away, leaving the job of raising and feeding of their young to their hosts. The cowbird is not the only absentee mother. More than 20 species of ducks occasionally lay their eggs in another's nest. One game biologist recorded that 13 different female redheads laid eggs in the same nest and as many as 87 eggs have been found in a single "dump" nest.

Needless to say, we sort of develop a dislike for this kind of irresponsible behavior among these birds. If we had the chance, we perhaps would like to smash the eggs of such birds who flee their homemaking jobs. However, the more we reflect on this unsavory situation, the more we realize that we are often guilty of the same maneuvers. There is an expression that sums it up among the human family—"Let George do it." We want to see a lot of things happen but we are unwilling to make them happen. We want the schools and the church to straighten out our kids if we have been unable to handle them at home. We want good, clean, efficient government without having to get involved more than at the ballot box. We've all got lots of ideas of how to improve society, if only someone else will hatch them and develop them. We curse the darkness, but are hesitant to light a small candle and hold it high. For too long we have been willing to lay eggs in someone else's nest, whether it be government, school, church, or law enforcement; and then we sit on the sidelines and hope some big mama will hatch them and raise them.

The abbreviation for the great United States is simply U.S., which spells "us." This nation will be no better than we are as individuals. Only when we pick up our shovels of responsibility and carry our own load will we be delivered from the impending tragedy of the "let George do it" slackers.

As World War I was ending, C. E. Montague, Manchester journalist, warned his countrymen that reconstruction would not come by "congress, conference, or general committee, or subcommittee, or any other expedient for talking in company instead of working alone." The individual has a job to do, he said—"To get down to work, whoever else idles; to tell no lies, whoever else may thrive on their use—to take less from your world than you give."

I am glad that not all birds operate like the cowbird. If they did, there would soon be no birds to watch nor songs to greet the dawn at your breakfast table.

A Faulty Foundation

No other foundation can anyone lay than
that which is laid, which is Jesus Christ.
1 Corinthians 3:11

The perfume of spring was in the air and the expectancy of
new life was the mood of the day. On this day which the
Lord had made there was a mother robin settled in her neat
nest, proud of her batch of blue-colored eggs. She had gotten
an early jump on spring and was setting on her eggs before
many of her neighboring cousins had even finished their
building projects. She was delighted with the progress of her
expected family. She had visions of little birds stretching
their necks at lunch time and beating their wings in
anticipation of their first trial flight.

But a few days after this very promising day some strange
movements began to happen in that backyard hedge where
the robin's nest was resting. The nest was secured to some
buds near the top of the hedge. The spring rains and the
kissing sun had caused the bushes to come alive and begin to
reach out their branches toward the sky. The buds opened,
the shoots stretched, and the nest began to move. The south
side of the nest was being elevated faster than the north side.
It was slowly being upset in the days that hastened by. The
eggs began to roll one morning and dropped to the ground.
The promise of life was encased in the tomb of those little
eggshells that would never be hatched.

Mother robin had made a mistake. She had secured her
nest to an unstable foundation. The foundation for her
hopes for new life was unreliable. Her nest was well made
and substantial. But it did not serve well, because of the
moving base upon which it was built.

41

Man, too, has difficulty in building life on a predictable platform. He has been known to use the building blocks of knowledge, friends, material possessions, security insurance, and a host of other mixes in an attempt to make an abiding foundation. He then proceeds in erecting a superstructure that is very impressive. But storms do come. Every house is tested sooner or later. Maybe it will be the flashflood of a falling economy. Perhaps the ill winds of sickness will howl around his house. Perhaps the termites of indulgence will slowly eat away the fiber of the house. It will be tested.

Jesus encouraged life-builders with these words: "Every one then who hears these words of Mine and does them will be like a wise man who built his house upon the rock; and the rain fell, and the floods came, and the winds blew and beat upon that house, but it did not fall, because it had been founded on the rock" (Matthew 7:24-25).

In Jesus Christ I have the assurance of sins forgiven, the hope of life eternal, and the abiding presence of God for my daily walk. That is sure stuff. I can bet my life on it and build my dreams on it. The Swiss Roman Catholic theologian Hans Küng said, "The church has one Word, and that Word is Jesus." He is the only lasting foundation.

"My hope is built on nothing less
    Than Jesus' blood and righteousness;
No merit of my own I claim,
    But wholly lean on Jesus' name.
On Christ, the solid Rock, I stand;
    All other ground is sinking sand."
        —Edward Mote, adapted.

The Bumblebee

With God all things are possible.
Matthew 19:26

Bees are always fascinating to busy boys. Because they sting, they present a challenge to young lads who desire to flirt with a little danger. So, during the growing-up years, most young boys have tried collecting bugs and bees and have also been the victims of beestings.

I remember romping in the clover fields, catching butterflies and bumblebees. The bumblebee is a large, hairy, social bee, so named because he makes a droning sound. This noise comes partly by beating his wings and partly by a humming within his tracheal tubes. These bees produce a scant supply of honey, but they are very valuable to farmers since they are the only bees with proboscises long enough to reach inside the flower of the red clover. Without these bees this valuable crop would not be pollinated.

Once I read that bumblebees are a scientific oddity. Because of their body size, weight, and placement of small wings, they should not be able to fly. You might think they would need at least a long runway to get up enough steam and momentum for take-off. But the bumblebee knows none of these mathematical laws of flight, and he just takes off and flies.

Man is often grounded in life because he believes it is impossible for him to fly. Psychologists tell us that most people use about 10 percent of their true potential. That simply means that 90 percent of most people's abilities and talents go untried, unused, and perhaps totally undiscovered. We don't think we can do something, so we don't try. We fail once or twice and then build psychological barriers over which we dare not cross. We overanalyze ourselves to the point of paralysis. Unless it is proved beforehand that we can do it, we back off from challenges because we don't want to fall on our faces again. The old proverb "Nothing ventured, nothing gained" has been discarded by many.

If we just start doing what we know we should do, maybe we will surprise ourselves and be like the bumblebee. I read that bicycle riders find it easier to ride up a hill at night than during the daylight. Hills that seem impossible to negotiate during the day are conquered at night. At night the cyclist sees only a few feet in front of him and the faint light of his lantern presents the illusion that the hill is level or at least not too steep. He feels he can go a few feet more and so he goes on and on. In the daytime he sees the whole hill and it overwhelms him. Then his courage fails with the size of the problem and he walks up with his bike. Life is often that way.

The apostle Paul made a practice of concentrating on a power that was limitless in his life, and thus he did some nearly impossible things. He said, "I can do all things in Him who strengthens me" (Philippians 4:13).

The Turtle Toddles

He who endures to the end will be saved.
Matthew 24:13

Have you ever had a turtle race? Well, they are one of the slowest creatures on land that our Creator made. As children we used to catch many mud turtles and a few snapping turtles in the ponds and river near my hometown of Windom, Minnesota. Sometimes we would line them up and try to prod them into a race. It never worked very well, because the turtles were less than competitive. But we always thought of the fable about the hare and the turtle; and, consequently, the toddling turtle was an underdog whom we admired. The fable certainly had an unexpected ending. Whoever would think that the turtle could win? The rabbit was endowed with great speed, but was overconfident and goofed off along the way by resting and daydreaming. The turtle kept moving—slowly, tediously—and he went on to win the race.

Many people have won in life by just keeping at it. Seemingly impossible tasks have been accomplished by people who were determined to succeed even though they possessed ordinary talents. When things move slowly, it is so easy to quit because we see little progress. One of Satan's most formidable weapons is discouragement. He tries to fill our lives with the weight of weariness, so we will throw in the towel.

Whether writing a book or doing the dishes, you must do one page or one plate at a time. It may seem very slow, but persistence always pays off and the job gets done. When I see a turtle toddle, I think of a nursery rhyme:

One foot up and one foot down,
That's the way to London town!
You can take only one step at a time. Some go faster than others, but they all must do the same stepping. Pressing on is the way of perseverance. Jesus talked about enduring to the end—that is, keep going to your destination.

William Carey was a pioneer missionary in India. When the call came for him to serve there, every obstacle seemed to loom in his way. A lesser man would not have started at all. When, at last he arrived in India, death took one of his children. His wife lost her mind. Carey hung on. After a life of service and accomplishment, he was talking to his nephew about the possibility of his life story being written. He said, "If he gives me credit for being a plodder, he will describe me justly. Anything beyond this will be too much. I can plod. I can persevere in any definite pursuit. To this I owe everything."

The turtle can also plod. Slow though he is, he usually gets where he starts out to go. One morning after a huge snowfall a little five-year-old boy took a big shovel outside and began to work on the front sidewalk. A man came by and said, "What are you doing, son?" The lad replied, "I'm shoveling a path for my dad." The man looked at the smallness of the boy and the bigness of the job and said, "And how do you expect to do it?" The little guy straightened up and looked the man in the face and boldly declared, "By just keeping at it."

That is the way the turtle wins his race—and so can we!

I Will Not Quit

Therefore, my beloved brethren, be steadfast, immovable, always abounding in the work of the Lord, knowing that in the Lord your labor is not in vain.

1 Corinthians 15:58

It was one of those balmy spring days; winter had relinquished its domination as hints of spring were lingering in the breezes. It was the kind of weather when men and birds felt like working. A wren had staked out her claim in our backyard. She had chosen a decorative little house perched on a fence post. Now she was busy bringing in the twigs for a little cradle to hold the tiny eggs she would soon be laying. Occasionally she would stop for a solo performance of one of the sweetest songs that God gave to the fowl family. When she sang, it seemed as though all the other songs from birds in the trees and bushes around our yard served as a subdued accompaniment for this talented little soloist.

However, a problem arose that morning as she tried to get an extra-large twig into the small round hole of the birdhouse. She was trying the head-on approach. The twig was too wide. She pushed and pushed. It would not bend. Finally it dropped from her beak to the green grass below. I thought she would forget it and attempt smaller twigs. But she dove down, picked up the same piece, and failed again. She then paused for song time. And lo, back to the same twig she went. This time she maneuvered the twig in her beak so she was holding it close to one end. Up she went to the perch and proceeded to cock her head so the short end jutted

47

through the hole. And with deft head movements like those of a skilled hand she succeeded in getting the job done.

Somehow that wren seemed to know that failures are neither final nor fatal. She did not seem embarrassed when the twig dropped from her beak. She neither blushed nor put her head under her wing. She didn't even look around to see if someone had seen her goof. Rather she kept right on working—and singing.

That little winged creature taught me a lesson that day without putting it on paper, but delivering it from the pulpit of her perch. It was simply that to fail is no disgrace. Quitting without a struggle is! The tragedy is when the spirit wilts and is not willing to try blooming again.

There was a young lawyer in Springfield, Illinois, who ran for the Illinois Legislature and was defeated. He tried business and failed. He was elected to Congress in 1846, served one term, but was defeated when he ran for reelection. Next he tried to get an appointment to the United States Land Office, and he missed it. He became a candidate for the United States Senate and was defeated. When 1856 rolled around, he was a candidate for the vice-presidential nomination, but was beaten again. Each time he shook the dust off his feet and moved on, until finally his steps led up to the entrance of the White House. He entered and went down in history as one of the great presidents. His name—Abraham Lincoln.

I need it and so do you. The right to fail. I need to know that God will permit me to try again. God does not insist on instant success, but only that we be faithful. In the game of life, if I cannot score running up the middle, maybe an end run or a pass play might work the next time around. Thank God there is always a huddle to go back to and get another play from the Quarterback.

The Pretending Possum

Examine yourselves, to see whether you are
holding to your faith. Test yourselves.
2 Corinthians 13:5

It was early one morning in the wooded hill country of
western Wisconsin. Dew had dampened the earth. My
children were out on an expedition of discovery. Down near
a hawthorne hedge they had encountered a furry animal
with a ratlike tail and long pointed nose. On the underside,
this 20-inch body had a well-developed birth pouch like a
kangaroo. The animal appeared motionless as if very sick.
The boys got a stick and began to jab this strange looking
creature, but they got little response. As they moved back, the
animal seemed lifeless. When the boys revealed their
discovery to me, I told them about their find. It was an
opossum.

Opossums usually hunt their food by night and spend
their days sleeping in trees. Their tails can neatly wrap
around a branch. In some sections of our country the
American opossum is hunted with dogs. The meat is
considered a culinary delicacy, and the fur can also be
marketed.

The opossum has developed a tactic which has surprised
its finders again and again. He habitually feigns death when
frightened. This habit has given rise to the popular
expression "playing possum." Thus, shortly after my boys
left the spot where they had met the opossum, this little
animal scurried off for the tree country. My boys, too, had
been fooled by the antics of this clever member of the wildlife
family.

The opossum has skillfully developed the art of pretending. Man also does quite well at it. The opossum saves his skin by being a pretender. Man sooner or later loses his when he practices this game of deception. As little children we all had a lot of fun playing doctor, nurse, teacher, and thief. Especially at Halloween, dressed as ghosts and goblins, we masked our true identity and rollicked in the role of pretenders. All this childish play was harmless indeed. But occasionally we kept playing games far after they should have been dropped along with our toys and kiddy clothes. We did not take the example of Paul: "When I became a man, I gave up childish ways" (1 Corinthians 13:11). We keep on pretending—sometimes to hide our inferiority feelings, sometimes to cover a lie, sometimes to impress a fellow man, sometimes to escape reality. And this type of deception is deadly. It spawns a day of doom.

It happened recently in our government. Men pretended not to know about a wrongdoing. They played the part of the three little monkeys who had their hands over their eyes, ears, and mouth. But the truth surfaced. The game was over. Men's lives were shattered.

Nature gave the opossum the gift of pretending in order to protect itself. God gave the gift of being open and honest to man for his own protection. Pretending is not for people. Sincerity is the name of the game for man. In the days of the Grecian columns and statues, the dishonest workman would fill the flaws and cracks with wax so it looked perfect. The beating sun and driving wind would later reveal the imperfections. The work was not "sincere." That word means "without wax." God wants His children to be sincere. He wants us to be for real, not pretending to be something that we are not.

The Chameleon's Camouflage

Do not be conformed to this world.
                                    Romans 12:2

As a little boy, I always wanted a chameleon. I heard that they could perform the neat trick of changing colors. Naturally, I thought this type of pet would be the neighborhood attraction. Not only did the color-change feature appeal to me, but the pictures I saw of this weird-looking creature were like a page out of the prehistoric past. I discovered many lizards in the window wells of our old church building at home when I was a small lad, but never got my hands on a real color changer.

The name chameleon is popularly given in the United States to several lizards capable of the seemingly magical maneuver of color transformation. The lizard's appearance is less than beautiful, with a compressed body and a conical head which has bulging bug-eyes moving independently of each other. He clings to branches with clawed toes and a long, grasping tail. His tongue can dart out like a rubber jack-in-the-box as he snatches insects, his main food.

The ability of this animal to change colors takes place inside his thick lizard skin. Imagine, if you can, assorted cells like marbles in a jelly substance. Suppose they are yellow, black, and white. If all the yellows crowd to the surface, they will hide the other two colors. The surface appears yellow. The roving eyes of the chameleon are sensitive to certain wave lengths of light and their signals cause these cells to react in the skin. Other tiny colored bodies reflect colors from surroundings. This remarkable turncoat can blend into many backgrounds, but obviously his color changes are limited.

Man in a crowd can often become like a chameleon. We find it easier to blend in with our surroundings rather than appear peculiar or different. This trait in man is tragic. He becomes controlled by crowd behavior as he is squeezed into the mold of the majority. He loses his calling to be "a light set on a hill," which Jesus calls us to be. Discipleship means playing for the coach and not for the crowd. Therefore the Christian is often going to stand out boldly against the backdrop of the world's colors. There is one thing of which we are sure. Every great historic change has been based on nonconformity. In the area of good it is the nonconformist who has raised the level of life. The church has been pulsating with life when it has been dissatisfied and restless with the world in which it lives. The church has been weak when it has become comfortable and cozy with the world around it and has blended into it.

Man was not called to be a chameleon in the world. God calls you to march to His tune, and that might make you out of step with many companions; some might even think you peculiar. Henry Thoreau, a rugged New England individualist of the 19th century, said, "If a man does not keep pace with his companions, perhaps it is because he hears a different drummer. Let him step to the music that he hears, however measured or far away."

Dare to be a Daniel,
> Dare to stand alone.
Dare to have a purpose firm,
> Dare to make it known.

The Fantastic Fish

I was not disobedient to the heavenly
vision.

The salmon is a well-known fish, since it is a familiar source
of food for millions of people throughout the world. One of
the main types is the Pacific salmon. Perhaps the king of
several groups within this type is the Chinook, which
usually weighs about 20 pounds but has been known to
reach 70 to 100 pounds. This king salmon is a powerful
long-distance swimmer. It will sometimes venture far up
into the Yukon River for spawning—a distance of 3,000
miles from the sea, where it spends most of its life.

When the Pacific salmon feel the tug of the spawning
grounds they leave the ocean. Often they stop feeding in
their frantic drive to head back to the place where their lives
started. In this upstream swim they literally wear themselves
out leaping over falls, rapids, and rocks which tear into
them. They make spectacular jumps which are almost
vertical.

Their spawning ground is the same spot where the adult
fish were born. The female salmon prepares a nest in gravel
and sand with her tail and fins and deposits her eggs in it.
The male then fertilizes the eggs, after which the female
covers them with sand. The parents then swim away to die.
They fulfilled their destiny. In about two months the eggs
hatch, and the young salmon will live in the fresh water for
about a year and then will go downstream into the salt water
of the ocean. There they will grow from two to seven years
and then head back home, where the cycle of nature begins
again.

I watched a television show once that used the phrase "salmon people." They were given that name since they felt they had a definite destiny to fulfill. This purpose for which they were born must be accomplished before they return home to God in death. They are driven on relentlessly by the compelling sense of destiny. This inner urge can certainly multiply a man's effectiveness. The apostle Paul felt God's hand on his life in being an ambassador for Him. As he talks to King Agrippa, he tells him that he was not disobedient to the heavenly vision he received from the Lord. Paul lived with a feeling of mission.

In Ernest Hemingway's masterpiece, *The Old Man and the Sea,* the old man, Santiago, has gone out to sea. This is prior to the big battle with the big fish, which becomes the dramatic struggle of the novel. The stage is prepared for this contest when the old man has just caught his bait and is preparing for the main business of his life—fishing. He says, "Now is no time to think of baseball—now is the time to think of only one thing. That which I was born for. There might be a big one in that school." That is focusing life. That is giving our attention to the thing we think most important. That is getting to the main tent for the big show rather than wasting time in the side shows. Jesus said, "Seek first His [God's] kingdom" (Matthew 6:33).

The man who lives with a sense of destiny gets the job done. As Theodore Roosevelt said, "It is better to run the risk of wearing out than rusting out." That is true in the life of the Pacific salmon. Not a bad thing for people either.

I read of a surgeon who felt called by God to be a doctor when he was a young lad sheepherding in the hills of Montana. He felt a date with destiny. He became a great surgeon and his autobiographical sketch was this, "When a boy and God get all tangled up in a dream, anything can happen and usually does." Why not dream up a destiny?

Sticking the Neck Out

One thing I do, forgetting what lies behind
and straining forward to what lies ahead, I
press on toward the goal for the prize of the
upward call of God in Christ Jesus.

Philippians 3:13-14

Have you ever noticed that when a turtle wants to go some place, to move ahead, he sticks his neck out? That's right. He can't go anywhere as long as he pulls his head and feet into his shell. To be sure, he is relatively safe within those walls of fortification, but he stands still. The only way you get a true glimpse of the creature is when he decides to get moving.

It is said that James B. Conant, former president of Harvard, had a small replica of a turtle on his desk with the motto: "Consider the turtle, he never makes any progress unless he sticks his neck out." That's true of people too. When I reflect some more on that fable of the race between the rabbit and the turtle, I believe it is absolutely amazing that the turtle was willing to enter the race in the first place. It's great he didn't say, "Well, I could never win a race with anybody. I would look like a fool beside that speedster. All the other animals would laugh at me!" But he stuck out his neck and entered the race. Hooray for the turtle!

There is a poignant statement in *Rumor and Reflection,* by art critic Bernard Berenson. In writing about aristocratic classes, he says, "A class begins to decline when it begins to play for safety, for securing its privilege, power, wealth, and, while sitting tight on its money bags, opposes innovation." Corporately and individually this happens to unsuspecting people. We like to play it safe, so we don't stick our necks out and risk the danger of moving ahead. The turtle is almost impervious to attack within his shell, but on the move he is susceptible to attack. That is also somewhat true for people. But we are only really alive when we are moving—when there is a spirit of adventure, sacrifice, and engagement in some hazardous enterprises.

I've often thought—what would have happened if Jesus would have played it safe and not gone to the trouble spot of Jerusalem? What if Paul would have decided it would be the better part of discretion to give up preaching Christ because it could get him into trouble? What if the Pilgrims decided to sit it out in Holland for safety's sake?

The Lord of Life wants none of us to be timid folk that avoid the risk of reaching out. By trying to save your neck you might lose your soul. People often get what they go after. That is what they deserve. If you take a thimble to the ocean and scoop up a few drops, it isn't the fault of the ocean that you didn't get more. If you think life has shortchanged you, don't blame life. Christ wants you to live abundantly. But in order for that to happen you must be willing to stick your neck out and be a fool for Him.

The mother superior in "Sound of Music" tells Marie, who has left the convent:

"Climb every mountain, ford every stream,
Follow every rainbow, till you find your dream."

There is a risk to mountains and streams. But that is what life is all about. Let's again consider the turtle.

The Begging Bears

If any one will not work, let him not eat.
2 Thessalonians 3:10

It was my first trip through the Rocky Mountains in the Yellowstone National Park vicinity. My friend and I had purchased an old 1937 Ford and were pushing westward in the kind of freewheeling trip that young boys dream about. Our first encounter with the black bears of Yellowstone was one of surprise over their bold dispositions. A dust-covered mama bear ambled over to our old car and proceeded to place her big paws on the window sill of the car door. I moved back a bit in my seat as she peeked into our car with a twitching nose. We knew what she wanted. She was a roadside beggar, and she was insistent on receiving some kind of alms from us before she would retreat into the shade of the woods.

While small children, we often heard stories of the big bad bear. Lots of them are big, but few of them are bad. Most bears are extremely wary of human beings and will not even permit us to get a glimpse of them. The king of the bears in North America seems to be the very intelligent grizzly bear. He walks with dignity and with lordliness of carriage. The grizzly embodies the spirit of the wilderness and the grandeur of the West. However, now and then we hear of grizzly bears invading a campsite and occasionally injuring or killing people. People began to form opinions that indeed bears are bad and they should be exterminated. Not so. People have unsuspectingly and unknowingly caused the bears to do mischievous and sometimes harmful deeds to humans.

It can happen very innocently. Over the past century garbage dumps have changed the bears' eating habits. The dumps become a part of their lives and some bears seem to have an uncommon predilection for human foods when they once start eating them. That is true whether the food is in a dump or in the form of groceries stacked on a shelf in an open cabin. Accessible garbage is the chief cause of bear trouble. Also, many campers stop their automobiles to feed the bears. Over the years the bears become more bold in their begging. The bears become pests, no longer interesting wild creatures with natural habits.

A definite pattern has evolved. First the bears are functioning in the wilds, searching out food, living off the land. As they become tempted by human handouts, they begin cautiously to taste these new human foods. They like it. Soon they expect it from any passing auto or campsite. The bear's life style becomes one of begging without working for his food. A dependency develops and the bear soon demands handouts. Then the bear has evolved into a dangerous freeloader.

The blame for the bear problems rests in our laps, for we have subsidized them so heavily with foodstuffs that they have forsaken their natural securement of food in the wilds to the easier method of demanding it from people. In the process these same bears lose a degree of their health and vitality—getting lazy and fat and ornery.

The begging bear serves as a warning to all peoples. Receiving handouts without working for our daily bread always ends in disaster. Too many subsidies will starve the dignity that a man finds only in "paying his own way." A nation can be destroyed by giving it too much, and it will be on its knees, miserable, greedy, and sick.

The Pack Has a Plan

After this the Lord appointed seventy
others, and sent them on ahead of Him,
two by two, into every town and place
where He Himself was about to come.

Luke 10:1

The big bad wolf does not deserve his reputation. From
stories such as Little Red Riding Hood and The Three Little
Pigs we have grown up with a false conception as to the
character of this magnificent animal of the wilderness areas.
Possessing perhaps more intelligence than his cousin, the
dog, the wolf frequently mates for life and respects the den
and property of another wolf. Wolves travel in family
groups, educate their young, provide for their old, and never
kill needlessly. Biologists tell us that the wolf has been
nature's way of maintaining a balance among other wildlife.
Wolves, when left to nature, will attack only the weak and
the old, thus weeding out misfits from herds of wild sheep,
moose, caribou, and deer. When the wolf has been removed
by hunting and poisoning in certain areas, some of the other
wildlife has multiplied so rapidly that sickness and
starvation has set in.

The timber wolf may vary from 60 to 175 pounds and can
run for hours at about 20 miles per hour. The howl of the
wolf is described as horrible in the fairy tales of youth.
Actually, it is more of a haunting melody as a family of
wolves will gather for a concert before and after a hunt.
Besides the hunting song there is a distinct "call" when
mother wants to gather her family for an emergency.

Before a hunt, wolves will observe a herd and carefully

pick out their victims. Their hunting strategy is among the most clever of all the predators. Quite often they will employ a relay system for the chase, so that as one wolf tires, a fresh one moves in until the exhausted victim is run to ground. Consequently, they seldom chase the wind. They catch that which they pursue. I guess we might all agree that a good plan is usually productive.

Perhaps the use of a plan would be one of the wolf's contributions in lessons from the wild. Too often we launch out into a project without designing a definite intelligible plan which can carry the ideal into reality. Jesus warned His disciples about commencing to build a tower without first sitting down and counting the cost (Luke 14:28-30). He said that a man going into battle had better size up the enemy before he starts the war (Luke 14:31). And when Jesus sent out His disciples, He sent them out two by two, giving them explicit instructions as to their mission (Luke 10:1-12).

Jesus had a game plan. In the athletic events of today we hear much about game plans. Reporters quiz the coaches as to their plans and whether they changed them during the course of the contest.

Perhaps we all need to sharpen up our objectives of life. If there is no goal or plan, it is true, we will never be very disappointed when we fail, for we were striving for nothing anyway.

The Frenchman Voltaire said of the people of his day, "They are like empty ovens, always heating, but never cooking anything." Not much gets done under those conditions. Let us have a little talk with God, develop a plan of life under His purposes, and get on with it. Goals attained and the joy of accomplishment will be the result.

May the ways of the wolf inspire you rather than frighten you!

The Cardinal Sings

> . . . singing and making melody to the
> Lord with all your heart.
>
> Ephesians 5:19

In Sioux City, Iowa, we had some tall Chinese elms in our
back yard that had witnessed the history of many years. They
were getting a bit bald. The skeleton branches without leaves
reached for the sky. These dead limbs became the perfect
perch for many birds who enjoyed sitting high enough to see
a lot of the world beneath. In springtime the crows would
drop by now and then. All they seemed to get done was to
scold and scream at everything around. If I stepped outdoors,
they would quickly leave the perch, but they would always
give a few more words of criticism before they got out of
hearing distance. Crows are not my favorite bird by any
means. Their speech is as somber as their color—jet black.
Even though they may eat some harmful insects and
decaying materials, they remind me of people who go
around constantly picking on some dead issue.

But not only crows visited our place in springtime.
Occasionally a cardinal attired in joyous red would drop by
and present us with a concert of the most thrilling song that
a creature could sing. We always wished the cardinal would
stay longer, for his singing seemed to lift the whole tone of
nature. We, too, wanted to sing his notes of praise and
promise!

Sometimes I would reflect about my own song. With
shamed face I realized that far too often I had the mood of the
crow and did more scolding than singing. Our church
pulpits are too frequently filled with men in black robes

61

shouting only messages of doom and destruction. People will cringe under the verbal barrage but are seldom changed in their hearts. You don't scare people out of hell; you sing them into heaven. I read about an intern who stepped into the pulpit to deliver his first sermon. He was apprehensive. He hesitated for a moment and then he broke into a smile as he shared with the congregation a note that had been left on the pulpit Bible. "Give 'em Heaven!" it said. That is exactly what the cardinal does.

On the cross, Jesus could have complained about the injustice being done. He could have struck out with words of wrath. Instead He prayed for forgiveness for the people. He talked about the promise of paradise. He showed concern for His mother. It was a sermon in song. After a centurion had witnessed it all he exclaimed, "Truly this man was the Son of God!" (Mark 15:39). That's the way it happens. When Jesus Christ is lifted up in the beauty of His love, men are drawn unto Him.

Maybe we all ought to sing more and scold less. There is a story of two grasshoppers that fell into a bowl of cream. One of them complained and groaned over his plight, and he sank to the bottom and drowned. The other sang and cheerfully kicked his feet until the cream turned to butter, and he hopped away to freedom.

Life can be that way. A Swedish proverb says it well: Those who wish to sing can always find a song. Let's make room for more cardinals.

Getting Hooked

Watch and pray that you may not enter
into temptation.
                                    Matthew 26:41

It was a cold November evening after Jack Frost nipped the
pumpkins and shook the autumn leaves off the trees. The
refrigerated air filled the lungs and made a person desire to
step briskly. The moon was kissing the earth with soft
beams, and occasionally a great horned owl would pierce the
silence of the night with his melancholy hoot.

A friend was taking me coon hunting for the first time.
He quietly released his two dogs from their compartment in
the back of his station wagon. The dogs were excited, and
they bounded off trying to pick up the fresh scent of recently
made raccoon tracks. In a matter of moments they began to
bay with the characteristic deep prolonged barks of hounds
in pursuit of their quarry. I began to tingle with suspense. It
was a new kind of hunting. Usually a coon will scurry up a
tree when it appears that he cannot outrun his pursuers. But
on this night we could tell that the hounds were continuing
their running as the barking began to fade and echo in the
dark woods. It was then that my friend muttered under his
breath. I could sense that he was mad, and I knew not why.
Disgustedly he then said that the dogs were chasing deer
rather than coon. If it were a coon, it would have already
been treed.

We jumped into the car and headed around a section of
woods for the southern clearing. As we got out of the car, the
sound of the baying hounds was coming in more distinctly.
We knew they were headed in our direction after making a

big circle in the woods. My friend grabbed a chain from the back of his car, walked into the woods silently, and then waited on a well-worn deer path. Sure enough—we heard the pounding of hoofs on the hard earth and soon a panting deer, with tongue hanging out, came jumping by. A few yards behind were the two dogs, also exhausted. My friend shouted at the dogs. They stopped. He went over to them, grabbed the older dog, and, with one hand on the collar and the other wielding the chain, he beat the dog in a way that seemed merciless and cruel. When he looked at me he saw my startled expression. Then he said, "I had to do it. When these dogs once start chasing deer, they are no good for coon hunting. If I didn't break them tonight while I caught them in the act, they would be hopelessly hooked on deer."

Animals seem to get hooked on things which are not right, just like man. When we play with temptation we usually get clobbered by temptation and are caught in its evil meshes. The only hope seems to be a quick break. Things must be stopped before they become habits. I recall one of our chickens finding an egg that had somehow broken. She tasted it and evidently liked it. The next day she deliberately broke an egg. That is when the trouble really started.

We all must learn to nip bad things in the bud before they come into full bloom. It is much more difficult to destroy a full grown plant than a seedling. Dag Hammarskjöld spoke wisely about temptation in this way: "You cannot play with the animal in you without becoming wholly animal, play with falsehood without forfeiting your right to truth, play with cruelty without losing your sensitivity of mind. He who wants to keep his garden tidy doesn't reserve a plot for weeds."

I thought at the time that the dogs chasing deer wasn't too serious, but my friend knew better. He didn't want them hooked to a bad habit.

Coveting and Cougars

Keep your life free from love of money, and
be content with what you have; for He has
said, 'I will never fail you nor forsake you.'
                                    Hebrews 13:5

The mountain lion silently slices through the night
darkness on padded feet as he relentlessly stalks his prey. His
movement is a symphony of rippling muscles. There is
suspense in the air as this magnificent beast, like a loaded
gun ready to fire a lethal shot, closes in on its prey. There is a
mighty spring, the crush of steel jaws, a whimpering cry of
the victim—and then stillness invades the mountain country
again.

The mountain lion goes by many names—puma, cougar,
panther. He is the world's fourth-largest cat. Man has long
regarded the big cat with a mixture of awe, fascination, and
fear. The mountain lion is endowed with a combination of
power, intelligence, speed, and great beauty of form and
movement. Many tales designed to frighten humans have
been spun to create an air of mystery about this mountain
ghost. The fact is that the mountain lion is frequently shy
and avoids humans as far as possible. He is declared to be the
finest deer hunter in the world and is credited with keeping a
balance of wildlife populations in his domain.

There is a unique characteristic about the cougar from
which we can learn. He is somewhat of a loner and is highly
territorial. This means that he stakes out his claim and
resides in the boundaries he has established. There is a great
deal of respect among the lions as to the properties of others.
This insures against excessive hunting pressures by lions in

any given area. Males will maintain a range of 20 to 100 square miles. This range will intersect with smaller ranges of several females, which average around 50 square miles. The respect for each other's range keeps down the possibility of overpopulation.

One of man's problem areas is the coveting of another's property. "The grass is always greener on the other side of the fence" has plagued humans since Adam and Eve. Two of God's commandments deal with coveting a neighbor's property and another with stealing. We are urged in our catechism to "help him improve and protect his property." The covetous man should learn from the cougar that when he stakes his claim he should be satisfied and must not try to infringe on his neighbor's domain. Constantly coveting another man's property, possessions, and mate will cripple a man's soul and will ultimately climax in a crisis.

We must learn to enjoy what we have and rejoice also in the acquisitions of our neighbor, whether it be property or personal talent. Dr. Harry Emerson Fosdick said, "The psychologically healthy person rejoices in the excellence of others. Objectively interested in whatever he is giving his life to, he is glad when a musician, teacher, or administrator appears who is better than himself." That takes God's grace.

Deliver us, Lord, from cages of covetousness, and let us concentrate on the territory in which we find ourselves. Let us bloom where we are planted.

Looking for beauty in all things

Sweetness Seekers

Finally, brethren, whatever is true, whatever is honorable, whatever is just, whatever is pure, whatever is lovely, whatever is gracious, if there is any excellence, if there is anything worthy of praise, think about these things.

Philippians 4:8

Bees are beautiful! They seek sweetness and they find it. When the worker bee is a few weeks old, she is ready to forage for family groceries. Her marketing chores include the gathering of pollen, resin, water, and nectar from the flowers. A scouting bee returns to the hive after locating a good source of supplies, does a fancy dance to direct the workers to the right area, and then off they go on their collecting trip. The worker bee selects a flower and crawls down into its throat to suck up a drop of nectar with her long tongue. Chances are, she will also fill the baskets on her back legs with golden grains of pollen. Then she makes a beeline back home to the hive to deposit her rich find of sweetness.

Bees are discriminating in their choice of flowers, for they are looking for honey nectar. What they find is directly related to that for which they are looking. Another creature with wings is a garbage collector. It is the buzzard. The buzzard looks for that which is foul as it feeds on the dead carcasses of other animals. They often spread contamination, for they, too, find that for which they are looking.

I hope that I am more like a bee than a buzzard. It is so easy to concentrate on the faults and foibles of others and then engage in gossip. Looking for the virtue, kindness, and good deeds in others requires discipline and practice. Two men can look through the same bars; the one sees mud, the other sees stars. Two boys can be eating grapes; the one rejoices in the taste, the other complains because the grapes have seeds.

I remember reading of two men who were traveling on a train. They were talking and soon discovered they had both recently been in India. The one man had hunted tigers for the government in remote villages, and as he told his story the other man said, "That is peculiar, for I was in India for several years and never saw a tiger." He then added, "I was a missionary proclaiming the Gospel of Christ." His companion responded, "That is funny, for in all my years in India I never met a Christian." Well, each found that for which he was looking.

In his explanation of the eighth commandment Martin Luther said something very important about our neighbor: "Apologize for him, speak well of him, and put the most charitable construction on all he does." William Arthur Ward said, "Looking through the wrong end of a telescope is an injustice to the astronomer, to the telescope, and to the stars; likewise, looking at our neighbor's faults instead of his attributes gives us an incorrect conception of ourselves, our neighbor, and God."

Jesus saw so much good in people and He drew it out of them. Consequently He was optimistic and hopeful. Our world today needs people who are more like honeybees than buzzards.

Flight Plans

Even the stork in the heavens knows her
times; and the turtledove, swallow, and
crane keep the time of their coming.

Jeremiah 8:7

I was sitting on a hillside rather pensively staring into the sky. The many-hued leaves were being lifted by the wind from their summer perches and were fluttering helplessly to the ground. Red-winged blackbirds were flocking impulsively on bush and tree. Nature seemed restless. Winter was approaching, and the world seemed to be shaken.

Was all life departing from the hillside on which I sat? Was I on a dead-end street? Was I to be left alone to wander aimlessly as nature was marching to its destiny, with the seasons playing musical chairs? Then my eye caught sight of a lone duck winging his way through the boundless sky. He was moving south, driven by some persistent urging within. He was alone at that moment, but he must have known where he was going. That duck stirred longings within my soul.

When migration is miraculously in motion across the autumn skies, something must be whispering "move" to most of the feathered creatures. They obey this instinctive voice. Scientists are still puzzled as to these uncharted flights. Inside the bird there seems to be a complex computer that is programmed by the Creator.

Eggs from storks that always migrate over the Strait of Gibraltar after nesting in western Europe were taken from the nest and kept warm until they could be hatched out by storks in eastern Europe. The matchlings grew to full storkhood and were seemingly content with their foster parents. Yet when migration time came and the foster parents headed for the Dardanelles Straits—as storks from eastern Europe do and always have done—the young birds headed in another direction—west—by themselves, flying across northern Europe and then crossing the Strait of Gibraltar, as instinct bade them.

Birds are amazing in their migratory exploits. A tiny hummingbird that measures under four inches flies over 4,000 miles—Alaska to Mexico. People tell of robins and purple martins that sometimes come back to their same nesting ground in consecutive springs. Yet man seems to be able to get lost with maps, compasses, and other equipment supposedly aiding him in reaching his destination.

Jesus said that man was of more value than the birds of the air. If that is so, will He not through the subtle shoves and beckonings of His Spirit guide my steps aright? The psalmist simply said, "He leads me" (Psalm 23:2). God has never reneged on His promise to provide guidance to one who is willing to be led.

I walked from the hillside that day with a song, for I felt that God was watching over me. My life was not like that of a squirrel in a cage, going round and round, getting nowhere fast. Rather it is a journey, and God is all wrapped up in it. Just as surely as He guides the big goose with his haunting honks and the little hummingbird with his helicopter spin, He will also guide me.

The poet, Robert Browning, saw it, felt it, and expressed it in this way:

I see my way as birds their trackless way,
I shall arrive! What time, what circuit first,
I ask not: but unless God send His hail
Or blinding fireballs, sleet, or stifling snow,
In some good time, His good time, I shall arrive:
He guides me and the bird. In His good time.

71

Lingering Too Long

Do your best to come before winter.

2 Timothy 4:21

No snow had descended from the fleecy clouds that had been drifting across the sky ever since fall was yielding to winter. The fields were bare, and shelled corn and soybeans lay scattered in areas that had not been plowed. Cold as it was, some ducks lingered and loitered in the northland, for the food was good in spite of the frigid temperature. There was one spot in the nearby lake that they managed to keep open. However, the mercury plunged on a lonely winter night as a storm system moved in. By morning the ducks were imprisoned by the ice that had closed in on their legs until they were hopelessly gripped in its death lock. There was only one thing to do. That was to die. Soon they would be food for the wandering fox who would venture out onto the ice for a dinner of cold duck. It was simply a matter of staying too long in the north country. There had been plenty of opportunity to head south, but the ducks procrastinated.

There is an interesting parallel in the life of the apostle Paul. He is in prison, nearing the end of the line, old age taking its toll. But he is busy writing letters of encouragement and God's truth. He writes two letters to Timothy, a close young friend. He longs to see him again. It is cold and dreary in prison, so Paul asks Timothy to bring his coat and some books when he comes to visit him in Rome. At the end of the letter Paul throws in a little comment that ought not be overlooked. He says, "Do your best to come before winter."

Why should he come before winter? Well, navigation on

the Mediterranean would be closed then. Weather would be bad. If he did not drop what he was doing, Timothy would not get there until the following year, and that may be too late. I wonder what Timothy did? Do you suppose he packed his bags and took off immediately? What if he had waited and left the following year, only to find that Paul had died during the cold winter?

We all need to cultivate the habit of responding now. We need to grasp opportunity when it knocks, for it has a way of knocking for the last time. Sometimes at funerals I find people wanting to say something to a dead body that can no longer hear. The poet said it well:

Bring me all my flowers, please, today;
    Be they pink, or white, or red;
I would rather have one blossom now
    Than a truckload when I'm dead.

Our children and friends need us now. We can't put them in a deep freeze for some more convenient day. Misunderstandings must be settled now before the infection grows deeper. Whittier penned wisdom when he wrote:

For of all sad words of tongue or pen,
The saddest are these: It might have been!"

Jesus emphasized the importance of the NOW in His ministry. Now is the day of salvation. Tomorrow may not come.

There is a season in everyone's life when good flying time must be heeded before it is too late. We dare not postpone important decisions and play with crucial choices. At the first urging of God's Spirit let us rise and move in the direction of His leading.

A Single Sparrow

I am like a lonely bird on the housetop.

Psalm 102:7

Winter had unleashed a mighty blast with frigid cold and waves of snow beating on the fertile fields of Iowa. Cattle and the birds of the field fell victim under its merciless attack. The toll of creatures was heavy. One farmer told me that he even found sparrows lying dead near his barn. But he was quick to add, "They are a nuisance and we were glad to get rid of some of them."

Sparrows have never held a very high rank among their feathered cousins. Man has usually looked upon them as pesky little creatures without much class or color. In early days they were sometimes used for food. They would crowd them together on a stick and roast them like marshmallows. They would then be dipped in sauce and the vendors would peddle them in the market place. Scripture says, "Are not two sparrows sold for a penny? And not one of them will fall to the ground without your Father's will. But even the hairs of your head are all numbered. Fear not, therefore; you are of more value than many sparrows" (Matthew 10:29-31).

Man can easily dismiss little things as being relatively unimportant. God doesn't. So, when God wants to let man know that He cares about him, He takes the sparrow and uses this little bird as an example. If God so cares about the birds—surely He cares about me.

Everything is important to God.

Charles Gabriel wrote a gospel song which affirms this concept very tenderly:

Why should I feel discouraged,
   Why should the shadows come,
Why should my heart be lonely
   And long for heaven and home,
When Jesus is my portion?
   My constant Friend is He:
His eye is on the sparrow and I know
     He watches me.

We all need to learn the Gospel of little things, for they are important. It is easy for a man in the grip of power to look down from dizzy heights and see little people who seem so insignificant. It is so easy to look at little tasks and do them shabbily, for they seem so unimportant. It is so easy to look inward and see so little self-worth. Sparrows and people—yes, they are both important to God.

Life is really an accumulation of little things—little decisions, little deeds, little opportunities. And Jesus asks you to be faithful with them all. He took some little men, in the eyes of the world, and molded His first cabinet. Those twelve shook the world. Jesus took the little lunch of a small lad and fed a multitude. Size must never be confused with significance. This Jesus asks you and me to treat all people with respect for they were created in His Father's image. We should clean up our picnic spot by the lake as carefully as the big government requests a large industry to clean up their pollution. Faithfulness to God in the little things which are mine to give and to do measures up to faithfulness in much.

She Came Back Home

I will arise and go to my father.

Luke 15:18

The wild mallards in my back yard lived the good life. I had purchased several of these magnificent ducks in the early spring and had clipped their wings so they were unable to fly. All their wants were provided in the yard, where there was a pond and where grain was supplied each day. They became very tame and seemed to enjoy the bustle of life where the children played. Other pets became a part of the family, and the ducks mingled freely with all of them. As summer slipped by, their wing feathers were growing out again. They flapped their wings more frequently. Soon there were trial flights around the back yard.

The sound of migrating geese was heard in the crisp fall evenings. The ducks were getting restless. Something inside them seemed to urge them to the skyways. During the autumn days their flight patterns increased daily as they went farther and farther from home. But they always came back to the shelter, food, and familiar surroundings of the place they called home.

Hunting season opened. The ducks were not aware of this perilous time. What I was afraid of happened. On a certain evening one of the mallard hens did not return. Was she shot out of the skies as she flew over the Missouri River? Did she find some migrating ducks and decide to join them in their southern trip? Whatever the case, she was gone. Then one day I looked out our house window and counted the ducks waddling in the back yard and was astonished to discover they were all there. I ran outdoors and saw the mallard hen that had been gone. However, her wing tip was dragging on the ground. At closer inspection it was very evident that it was broken. Apparently she had been shot.

How she found her way back home, I don't know. All I know is that it must have been a hard journey, for ducks aren't made for walking. She must have thought home was worth coming back to.

Jesus told the story of a prodigal son who left his father's house in search of something he thought was better than home. But his search was misdirected, and his loose living ended up with him sitting down to a banquet of consequences. He had sown wild oats, and the harvest of destruction was more than he bargained for. He was now penniless and hopeless. He began to dream of home. And he began to realize that home was worth going back to. The boy had known the love of his father, and that love was the compelling force that led his footsteps back to a new life at home. It was a hard journey, but he made it.

I remember reading *The Call of the Wild,* by Jack London. Buck, the wolf dog, was a creature of the wild. His wild heritage would pull strongly against his loyalty to his master, John Thornton. There was the constant struggle within to run away and yet also to stay. Buck had shared many firesides and much food with his master. Here is the way it is described: "Deep in the forest a call was sounding, and as often as he heard this call, mysteriously thrilling and luring, he felt compelled to turn his back upon the fire and the beaten earth around it, and plunge into the forest, and on and on, he knew not where or why; nor did he wonder where or why, the call sounding imperiously deep in the forest. But as often as he gained the soft unbroken earth and the green shade, the love of John Thornton brought him back to the fire again."

That is what love can do. The duck, the son, the dog came back home, for love was waiting. Let us all make our homes a place that is worth coming back to. And God is waiting, too. Hurry back home where you belong.

The Stealing Skunk

Truly, truly, I say to you, he who does not
enter the sheepfold by the door but climbs
in by another way, that man is a thief and a
robber.

John 10:1

Our mother mallard duck was exhausted and somewhat
despondent. Three times she had attempted to raise a family,
and each time some intruder had worked his way into the
pen and destroyed the nest of eggs that contained the hope of
little ducklings. Mother duck gave up trying for the rest of
that summer season. My young sons joined the mother duck
in her frustration. They, too, had looked forward in great
anticipation to the hatching excitement and the fun of
watching a brood of ducklings play in the small pond of
water within the pen.

War was declared on the intruder, whoever he might be.
The first suspect was our cat. But cats are not known egg
snatchers. One day a rat was seen snooping around our
woodpile, and my boys promptly alerted me to the
possibility that our criminal had been found. The rat was
shot when he came up out of the woodpile to survey the
situation. But to our chagrin the eggs continued to be
broken. Finally the boys decided to set a trap, and they baited
it with a chicken egg. The first night the trap was sprung but
caught nothing. Suspense mounted as they reset the trap the
second evening. Upon rising early in the morning to see if a
thief had been caught, the boys rounded the corner of the
pen, and there they stared a skunk straight in the eyes. He
was caught by one leg and eyed the boys defiantly. The
mystery of the disappearing eggs had been solved.

The skunk is a predator. He is about the size of a cat. His body is elongated with an arched effect. The head is comparatively small with a blunt snout for sticking into other folk's business. On the forehead is a patch of white diverging into two lines that extend the whole length of the back and meet again in a bushy tail. The skunk has nocturnal habits, and his chief defense is a smelly discharge that can make anyone back up in a hurry.

Skunks are thieves. They break in without entering by the door, and they do it under cover of darkness. Satan is a skunk. He enters human life by every devious way imaginable. He climbs over the fence and burrows under the fence in order to steal from a man's soul. Peter says of him, "Your adversary the devil prowls around like a roaring lion, seeking some one to devour" (1 Peter 5:8). He is a predator. No friend will break into your house when you are on a trip. An enemy will. Friends enter by the door and only when it is opened to them. Not so with an enemy.

Consequently we are all subject to the attacks and invasions by evil, for Satan is constantly attempting his break-ins to rob and steal any good thing in our lives.

Jesus comes knocking. He wants entrance into our lives. He comes with gifts of pardon, peace, and power. He wants to establish residence in us and ward off the attacks of evil. He will protect us, His sheep, from Satan the stealer.

"Behold, I stand at the door and knock; if anyone hears My voice and opens the door, I will come in to him and eat with him, and he with Me" (Revelation 3:20).

Petting the Puppy

This is My beloved Son, with whom I am
well pleased.

Matthew 3:17

Many puppies have found their way into our house and
hearts down through the years. Some have romped in and
out at random. Others have been trained with tenderness and
discipline. In being a professor to puppies, I have learned
one truth quite dramatically. Puppies perform best when
they are petted. If a person becomes too critical in his
training of a puppy and tries to scare him into obedience,
nothing will result but a puddle on the floor where the
puppy cowers in fear. Certainly sternness needs to be
exercised, but it must be liberally sprinkled with pats of
affection when the young dog does his thing in the right
way. Whether it is in the area of housebreaking, heeling, or
hunting skills, the dog needs to be rewarded with a
compliment when doing his task properly.

Today in human circles we call it giving a "stroke." A
stroke is a unit of recognition, and it can be either verbal or
physical. All of us work best in the sunshine of approval. It
seems as though a human child at birth is given a vessel of
dignity and self-worth. Everytime we merely criticize or
condemn and scold we take a spoonful of confidence from
his bowl. Some young people have been scooped dry before
they reach adulthood. Only by proper stroking with
recognition and applause can we keep the bowl filled to the
adequate level. Without that they will sell themselves short
of their potential and will die with much of their music still
in them. They will be afraid of using their talent.

When Jesus was baptized by John in the river Jordan, there was a voice from heaven declaring, "This is My beloved Son, with whom I am well pleased." Jesus had been a carpenter so far, and now He was to begin His public ministry. At such a time Jesus, as true man with human feeling, received a beautiful stroke from His Father in heaven. No doubt it gave Him a lift of confidence.

If a man sees nothing in himself of potential and worth, he will be most miserable. This feeling of inferiority is a serious handicap to overcome. If a man finds himself in such a hole, he will usually need the encouragement of another who, by word and action, will demonstrate belief in him. One of the saddest lines in Scripture is that of the psalmist: "No man cared for my soul" (Psalm 142:4 KJV). Over and over again Jesus lifted people to a new sense of self-respect. Someone has wisely said, "The worst way to improve the world is to condemn it." How true! And it applies also to a person. As Jesus stood before a sinful person one day, He said, "Neither do I condemn thee; go, and sin no more" (John 8:11 KJV). She had missed the way. He did not minimize her sin, and neither did He minimize her possibilities. Even though He was well aware of her shameful past, Jesus saw that her future could be different. One person said of Christ, "In the company of sinners He dreamed of saints."

Maybe someone needs to hear a compliment from you today. Maybe someone longs to hear, "I believe in you." If puppies are trained by petting, perhaps sinners will become saints through the strokes of love.

Prime importance . . . materialistic world?

Family First

> He took them the same hour of the night, and washed their wounds, and he was baptized at once, with all his family.
>
> Acts 16:33

The Black Hills have become a favorite vacation spot for our family. There is plenty of creation there. Rock formations, pointed pines, forest flowers, rushing streams—all vie for your attention. It is a good place to take off the shoes of business and stand in awe of God's magnificent creation. Elizabeth Barrett Browning captured the feeling in her verse:

> Earth's crammed with heaven,
> And every common bush afire with God,
> But only he who sees takes off his shoes—
> The rest sit round it and pluck blueberries.

On a particular exploratory hike my children came upon the home of a squirrel family. It was a fine house built into a rugged pine. Needless to say, they had to climb up and check on whether the squirrels were at home that day. Their anticipation was fulfilled as they reached in and felt the downy fur of several little creatures. They reasoned that mother squirrel would not miss one of her young ones, and so a kidnapping took place. Back at camp they excitedly showed me their acquisition. Their smiles turned to soberness when I announced that the little fellow must be brought back to his family. However, they did coax me into keeping it with them till the following day, when they would return it.

The next day the sad journey was made by two of my children with the little guy they had hoped to have as

84

another pet. Soon they arrived back after their mission. But the squirrel was still in their possession. The problem was that sometime during the evening mother squirrel had come home and discovered the abduction. She feared for the rest of her family, and so she abandoned her home quickly, moving the entire family to some distant new home where they would not be found. There was only one thing to do now. My children would have the responsibility of raising this young squirrel. This they did with gladness. And a fine young pet he became.

Mother squirrel had taught me quite a lesson. Her family was much more important to her than her house. What happened to her children was of prime importance. Living in a materialistic world we humans can forget that. We sometimes worry more about the house and possessions than the children who live there. If one of my sons were riding his bike, and I heard the crash of a car running into the bike, would it not be ludicrous to run out to the street where a battered bike lay beside a broken body and exclaim, "What happened to the bike?" Maybe we are too concerned about buildings, civilizations, and economics and too little concerned about people. God keeps the whole show going only to do something for man—to bring him into the fellowship of the family of faith.

Edwin Markham wrote:
> We are blind until we see
>   That in this human plan
> Nothing is worth the making,
>   If it does not make the man.
>
> Why build these cities glorious,
>   If man unbuilded goes.
> In vain we build the work,
>   Unless the builder also grows.

Puppy Love

Love bears all things, believes all things,
hopes all things, endures all things.
1 Corinthians 13:7

We have always had dogs in our family. There have been big
ones and small ones, registered ones and mongrels,
purchased ones and lonely strays. A good dog may be called
man's best friend, but it seems even more that dogs were
made for little boys. And each dog that crosses a boy's life
leaves a footprint of some kind on his heart.

I remember well my father and I burying a little cocker
spaniel that had been a member of our family for several
years. We dug a hole in the soft, damp earth, and with
studied gentleness my father put the body to rest. The grave
was then blanketed with the black earth, and another cycle
in the eternal miracle of creation had come to a close. A tear
hung in my eye, for I had lost a loyal friend.

As I grew older I continued to enjoy the presence of dogs.
When I finished the seminary, I purchased a stately white
German shepherd pup. This dog developed a fierce loyalty.
One day, while I was fishing a few hundred yards from
shore, this young pup was pacing up and down along the
shoreline. Not long thereafter I saw a white form approaching the boat, coming like a big muskrat in the water.
It was my pup. By the time he reached the boat he was totally
exhausted and he just about collapsed when I lifted him into
the boat's bottom. But the strong desire that he had to be by
my side was a memory that has been etched permanently
into my mind.

I have often wondered what it is about humans that dogs

like so well. Whatever it is, it can only be broken by death itself. Dogs don't seem to care whether their master lives in a cave or in a castle. They will stick by your side whether you feed them scraps or the latest brand of canned red meat. The mongrel following at the heels of a tramp is just as devoted as the pampered pedigree pet of a society lady. The conclusion that I have reached is that a dog's love is not conditioned by what he is going to get out of a relationship. All he asks is to belong, and he finds great happiness in that alone.

Man's love is so easily polluted. We so often love in order to get something. Peter revealed this problem when he asked Christ, "Lo, we have left everything and followed You. What then shall we have?" (Matthew 19:27). We are so often guilty of worshiping because we want something from God. Would we follow Christ if He led us into poverty—if He led us into the valley of suffering—if He led us to a cross?

There is an old story about a strange woman in the early days of Christianity who went about the city streets with a pail of water in one hand and a flaming torch in the other. She would shout as she walked along, "Oh, that I could douse the flames of hell and burn the furniture of heaven so that man would love God for Himself alone." God's love is a beautiful thing. He loves me, not for what I have achieved or for what He can get out of me. He just loves me—period. Oh, that I might love Him for just being what He is—a great and good Heavenly Father.

More love to Thee, O Christ,
    More love to Thee!
Hear thou the prayer I make
    On bended knee.

Snakes and Trains

Be sober, be watchful. Your adversary the devil prowls around like a roaring lion, seeking some one to devour.

1 Peter 5:8

Snakes and trains have somethings in common. They are both long and narrow and they both must know where their tail end is! As a little boy I was fascinated by this twosome. Frequently I would go in search of snakes. They were good for little except for the fine fun of scaring both the neighborhood girls and also my mom. But catching snakes was an art for a small boy. I would chase them through the long grass and the garden foliage until they would crawl under a thick mat of grass or under a garden rock. Quite often they would be completely hidden except for their tail, which did not get covered. The snake, no doubt, surmised that he had escaped his pursuer—only then to feel a tug on his tail. Soon he was pulled out of hiding and was captured. His undoing was his negligence in noting where his tail end was. Forgetting to care for it was a catastrophe!

The train also can have identical problems. As a lad I spent many moments near the bustling railroad tracks through Windom, Minnesota. The main Omaha-Twin Cities line kept many trains moving through my hometown. As I walked the rails, I noticed signs with the series of numbers 100, 125, 150. What were they? Certainly trains in that day could not travel those speeds or they would have flown right off the tracks. Years later I was made aware of the fact that these were signs that designated the number of car lengths to the switch. If it was a long train, the engineer was not able to see the end of it; and if he were pulling off on a side track, he must know whether his tail end had gotten off the main track. Therefore, if an engineer knows the number of cars in his train and comes to one of these signs, he will know whether his caboose is on the siding or not. If the engineer does not know where his caboose is at all times, he might be the cause of a collision as another train comes rolling down the main track.

People must also know, as it were, where their tail ends are. Sometimes a person can become so concerned about the body and its needs that he forgets all about the sustenance of the soul. The person outruns his soul and one day finds the soul is starved and Satan has caught him. It is easy for a teacher to open the throttle and race down the tracks with the mentally sharp students, and the slower students in the caboose are neglected and end up in a mental collision. Parents have a great temptation in running ahead of their children without taking time to talk about the hurts and dreams of their young ones. They may think everything is okay back in the caboose, but often there are wrecks, because they didn't know where the caboose was, spiritually and maturingly. The church has also occasionally been guilty of roaring down the theological track, tooting its horn, without knowing where the people in the pew are. The preacher might be proclaiming social issues while the people have not resolved personal issues. Degrees of saintliness might be the subject while the brakeman in the caboose has not even caught up with the simplicities of right and wrong.

Well, we can't get rid of the caboose. It is a part of the whole train. If not handled wisely, it will be the making of a first-class wreck. So it is in life. The snake and the train warn us to keep an eye on the tail end.

The Floating Falcon

> They who wait for the Lord shall renew
> their strength, they shall mount up with
> wings like eagles, they shall run and not be
> weary, they shall walk and not faint.
>
> Isaiah 40:31

I lay on my back on a hillside, shading my eyes from the sun, watching a hawk glide effortlessly in the sea of blue sky. The bird seemed so free. Then, without any noticeable movement of the wings, the hawk started spiraling upward as though riding some invisible escalator to another story of the heavens. The hawk was getting a free ride on an updraft of air movement. These air currents are similar to air being pushed up an elevator shaft, and the hawk knew how to use them.

While riding in a small airplane, I was made aware of turbulant air happenings in the heavens. It was one of those days when unsettled weather was acting like a man with an upset stomach. The little craft all of a sudden was thrown upward, as if tossed by the hand of a giant. Yet we could see nothing in the invisible air all around us. The next moment the plane would drop many feet, as though the floor had dropped out of the sky.

The hawk, instinctively perhaps, and with much practice, knew how to stay in the corridor of updraft. He could relax, knowing the wind would support him. He could enjoy it and revel in the exhilaration of gliding maneuvers without so much as flapping a wing.

Sometimes I get the notion that with the wings of faith we could soar in the air patterns of God's rich grace. I think we often struggle when we should relax. I believe we worry when we should be resting. We often seem to fight the wind rather than be lifted by it. The late professor Halford Luccock told of speaking at a college where a young man came up after the presentation and said that religion is all moonshine. Luccock thanked him for that description. Then he proceeded to ask the student if he had ever been to Panama and watched a 22-foot tide come in. The young man said, "No, but what has that to do with religion?" Luccock told him that moonshine—the pull of another world, an unseen but resistless force, was lifting those billions of tons of water. Religion is unseen and real like moonshine in its measureless lift to life.

When we learn to relax and trust God, then we start to learn the art of floating like the falcon, and it is exciting!

Sidney Lanier, American poet, was in his mid-30s when he developed tuberculosis. He knew his life would be shortened. He went to the coastland into milder climate. There, looking across the marshes and seeing wildlife at its best, he wrote one of his finest poems:

As the marsh-hen secretly builds on the watery sod,
Behold I will build me a nest on the greatness of God:
I will fly in the greatness of God as the marsh-hen
    flies
In the freedom that fills all the space 'twixt the marsh
    and the skies:
By so many roots as the marsh-grass sends in the sod
I will heartily lay me a-hold on the greatness of God.

Wings of Power

They who wait for the Lord shall renew their strength, they shall mount up with wings like eagles, they shall run and not be weary, they shall walk and not faint.

Isaiah 40:31

We were paddling our canoe in the Minnesota-Canadian boundary waters. Nature was having an open house as we quietly glided along the shoreline of a secluded lake. Beavers were at work building dams on small inlets; song birds were gathering in concert; a tall crane stood on sentinel duty by the water's edge; a cow moose and her young calf scrambled out of the weedy shallows. But suddenly there was a scream in the blue heavens above. We were intruders to this territory and someone didn't like our presence. We lifted our eyes and saw a sight that made my heart skip a beat. There on powerful wings was soaring the regal and defiant bird called the bald eagle. The flight was effortless, and when the wings moved, they spelled out superb strength and skill. It was little wonder that our country chose this bird as an emblem for its people forging out a new life in a strange land.

The eagles usually mate for life, and they build nests which stagger the mind. Some have measured eight to nine feet in diameter. As they add to them year after year, these nests have become 15—20 feet deep. The eagle's swiftness was praised in Biblical passages, and both the golden and bald eagles have been clocked in power dive spurts at around 120 miles per hour.

However, these kingly birds have a tenderness which matches their strength. They guard their young with patient care. When the Israelites were making their way through the wilderness, the eagle became for them a sign of God's power and providence. In the song of Moses it is graphically portrayed: "Like an eagle that stirs up its nest, that flutters over its young, spreading out its wings, catching them, bearing them on its pinions, the Lord alone did lead him, and there was no foreign god with him" (Deuteronomy 32:11-12). In this description you can see the mother eagle arranging and rearranging the nesting material like a busy mother tidying up her house. The eaglets were doted over as she would shield them from blazing sun and stormy gales with her wings. Then would come a day when the little ones must try a solo flight. She would coax them with gentle shoves. Actually, they would be pushed from the nest as they trembled with fear. Now comes one of the most remarkable acts of nature. In recent years reliable observers have seen parent eagles doing what the Scriptural writer observed so long ago—that is, swooping under a floundering young one and bearing it up on her own back. In this way the mother bird would save the frightened fledgling from falling too fast to the rocks below, and it would be able to try its wings again.

The exquisite picture of Scripture is that God watches over His people as an eagle watches over its young. With the people of Israel, God pushed them out of the nest of Egypt and enabled them to try the wings of freedom. They had a destiny, and God was there to "bear them up on His wings" (cf. Exodus 19:4 KJV) again and again as they faltered on their flight to the Promised Land.

God still pushes His people out of their nests of security blankets, mediocrity, and stuffy tradition. He wants our spirits to soar beyond the earthbound nest and strive for the kingdom of heaven.

Watch an eagle in flight—watch her care for her young—then think of the strength and sustaining concern of the Lord.

The Shell Stretches

Grow in the grace and knowledge of our
Lord and Savior Jesus Christ. To Him be
the glory both now and to the day of
eternity. Amen.

2 Peter 3:18

Sea shells come in all sizes, shapes, and colors. Larger ones
can be held next to your ear, and you seem to hear the
whisper of waves lapping up against the ocean shore.
Colored ones are used for table decorations and some for
paper weights. Much of the fun is in collecting these
discarded bodies belonging to little animals of the sea world.
One of these shells is especially intriguing. It is that of the
pearly nautilus. In the spiraling shell of gradually enlarging
compartments a mollusk, likened to a snail, successively
lives as it grows larger and larger. It moves from one
chamber to another, until it is finally free, leaving behind its
shell. One of our famous American poets was fascinated by
this shell as he caught the imagery of the human soul
expanding and growing until someday it, too, would move
on. The poet was Oliver Wendell Holmes. The poem was
entitled, "The Chambered Nautilus." In it he wrote:

Build thee more stately mansions, O my soul,
    As the swift seasons roll!
    Leave thy low-vaulted past!
Let each new temple, nobler than the last,
Shut thee from heaven with a dome more vast,
    Till thou at length art free,
Leaving thine outgrown shell by life's
        unresting sea.

Never too old to grow

94

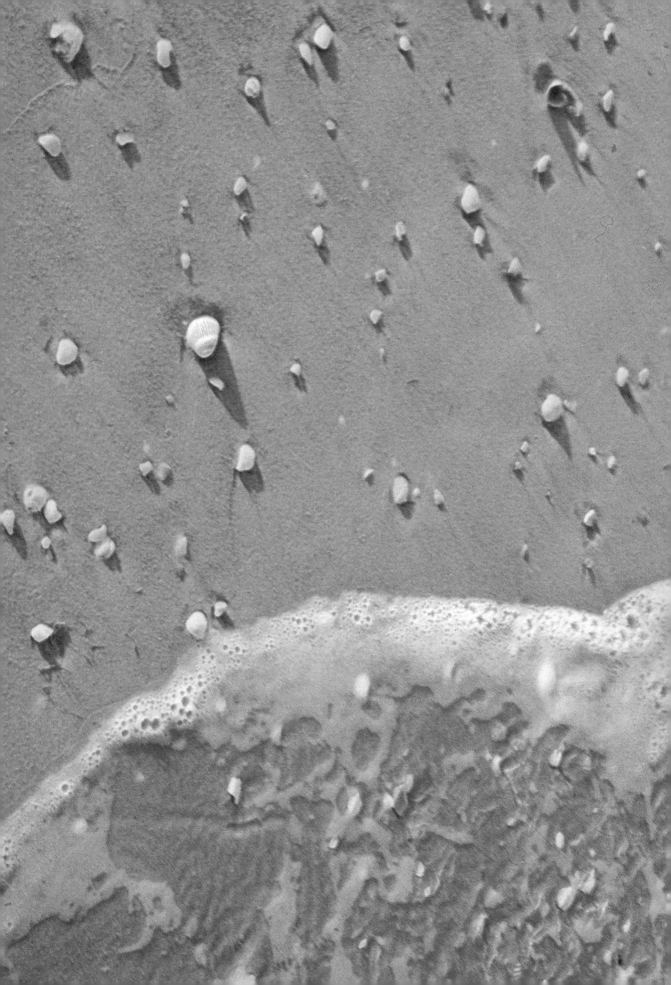

The nautilus speaks a sermon of growing until you vacate your body, the place of habitation. Too frequently the human spirit has its spurts of growth in younger years, but then withdraws in its shell and withers as older age approaches. Remember the themes you wrote in high school English composition? Normally, your stories followed a definite pattern. First was the introduction; next came the rising action and plot development; then was the climax, or turning point, when the story slowly unraveled, until you tacked on a fitting conclusion. Some think of life in that way. You have suspense and action until you are about 40. From that point it is downhill all the way until death's departure. Nonsense! Biologically, the body does reach a point of physical maturity after which it loses some of its vitality. But is not life more than body? The human spirit can continue to soar and grow until God calls us home. No man or woman should peak at 40. An old piece of wisdom says, "Grow old along with me, the best is yet to be." That's anticipation. That's expectancy. Grandma Moses, who started painting when most people start dying, serves as an example of the human spirit constantly growing. We need not crest like an ocean wave until the time comes when we make the final journey back to our homeland with the Father.

When William James celebrated his 70th birthday, a friend asked him if he believed in personal immortality. "Never stronger," he replied, "but more so as I grow older. Because I am just now getting fit to live!" That's great—growing and growing as God continues to prepare His people for a life larger and richer than man can begin to visualize or conceptualize.